TORNADOES

by Jaclyn Jaycox

PEBBLE
a capstone imprint

Published by Pebble, an imprint of Capstone
1710 Roe Crest Drive, North Mankato, Minnesota 56003
capstonepub.com

Copyright © 2022 by Capstone. All rights reserved. No part of this publication may be reproduced in whole or in part, or stored in a retrieval system, or transmitted in any form or by any means, electronic, mechanical, photocopying, recording, or otherwise, without written permission of the publisher.

Library of Congress Cataloging-in-Publication Data
Names: Jaycox, Jaclyn, 1983- author.
Title: Tornadoes / by Jaclyn Jaycox.
Description: North Mankato, Minnesota : Pebble, [2022] | Series: Wild earth science | Includes bibliographical references and index. | Audience: Ages 5-8 | Audience: Grades K-1 |
Summary: "Funnel cloud. Siren sounds. Take shelter! Tornadoes are a force of nature that can quickly spin across the land. Their powerful winds can cause lots of damage. But you can be prepared! Learn about tornadoes, pay attention to warnings, and stay safe"—Provided by publisher.
Identifiers: LCCN 2021042177 (print) | LCCN 2021042178 (ebook) | ISBN 9781663976994 (hardcover) | ISBN 9781666327076 (paperback) | ISBN 9781666327083 (pdf) | ISBN 9781666327106 (kindle edition)
Subjects: LCSH: Tornadoes—Juvenile literature. Classification: LCC QC955.2 .J39 2022 (print) | LCC QC955.2 (ebook) | DDC 551.55/3—dc23
LC record available at https://lccn.loc.gov/2021042177
LC ebook record available at https://lccn.loc.gov/2021042178

Editorial Credits
Editor: Ericka Smith; Designer: Tracy Davies; Media Researcher: Svetlana Zhurkin; Production Specialist: Katy LaVigne

Image Credits
Associated Press: Pavel Rahman, 25; Dreamstime: Menno Van Der Haven, 11, Orlando Jose De Castro Junior, cover, 3; Getty Images: Jason Persoff Stormdoctor, 13; NOAA Weather in Focus Photo Contest 2015: Francis Lavigne-Theriault, 14, Ken Engquist, 17, Ryan Lueck, 8; Shutterstock: Cammie Czuchnicki, 6, CiEll, 24, Designua, 7, Dustie, 23, dynamic (map background), back cover and throughout, Gino Santa Maria, 20, 21, J.J. Gouin, 27, John D Sirlin, 4, 16, lafoto, 29, Limitless Production Group, 19, Martin Haas, 5, Melissa Brandes, 22, Minerva Studio, 1, 9, 12, 26, pashabo, cover (logo), Photoguru73, 28, Rainer Lesniewski, 18, trgrowth, 15

All internet sites appearing in back matter were available and accurate when this book was sent to press.

TABLE OF CONTENTS

Swirling Storm 4

What Are Tornadoes? 6

Types of Tornadoes 12

Where in the World? 16

Tornado Aftermath 20

Staying Safe 26

Glossary 30

Read More 31

Internet Sites 31

Index 32

About the Author 32

Words in **bold** are in the glossary.

SWIRLING STORM

The sky is dark. A storm is forming. But it isn't just any storm. Clouds start to swirl. A **funnel** appears. It drops toward the earth. It's a tornado!

Tornadoes are a kind of natural **disaster.** They might last only minutes. But they can leave behind a lot of damage.

WHAT ARE TORNADOES?

Tornadoes are spinning **columns** of air. They are also called "twisters" or "cyclones." They form during thunderstorms called **supercells**.

A tornado touching down in Colorado

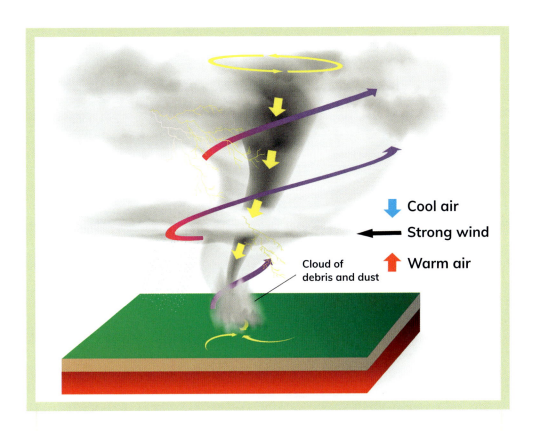

During a storm, warm, wet air rises from the ground. Cool, dry air falls from the sky. They meet. The wind changes direction. The wind starts to spin quickly. It looks like a funnel. The funnel drops from the clouds. If it touches the ground, the funnel becomes a tornado.

A wide tornado on the ground in South Dakota

Tornadoes are all different sizes. On average, they are 300 to 500 yards (274 to 457 meters) wide. But some are more than 2 miles (3.2 kilometers) wide.

You can't see wind. Water droplets make it possible to see a tornado. Tornadoes also pick up dust and **debris**. They can give tornadoes color. Some are white or gray. Others are black, red, or even blue.

Tornadoes travel across the ground. On average, they move at about 30 miles (48 km) per hour. Some move as fast as 70 miles (113 km) per hour.

Tornadoes may last only a few seconds. But some last more than an hour. Most are over in about 10 minutes.

TYPES OF TORNADOES

Many tornadoes form on land. But some form over water. And some move over water. When they are over water, they are called **waterspouts**.

Dust and debris swirl around the outer edge of a multiple vortex tornado.

Tornadoes can have several funnels. This kind of tornado is called a multiple **vortex** tornado. It can have as many as five smaller funnels.

There are different categories of tornadoes. Scientists use the **Enhanced Fujita (EF) Scale**. This measures a tornado's strength by wind speed. Knowing the real wind speed inside a tornado is hard. But scientists can guess. They base their guess on the damage a tornado causes.

An EF-4 tornado hit South Dakota in 2014.

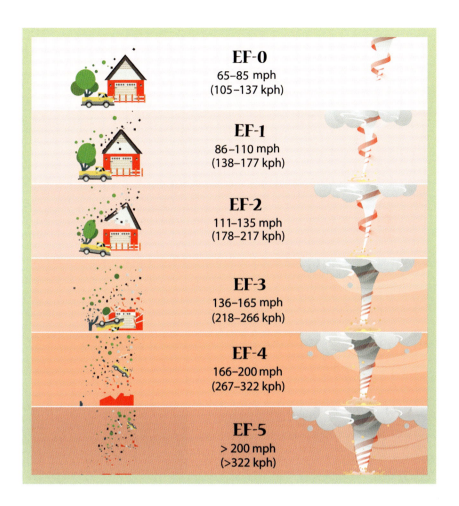

The weakest tornadoes are EF-0. They have wind speeds up to 85 miles (137 km) per hour. The strongest are EF-5. Their winds blow more than 200 miles (322 km) per hour.

WHERE IN THE WORLD?

Tornadoes can occur anywhere. But most happen in the United States. About 1,200 tornadoes hit the country each year. That's four times more than the rest of the world combined.

A tornado in Nebraska

TORNADO ALLEY

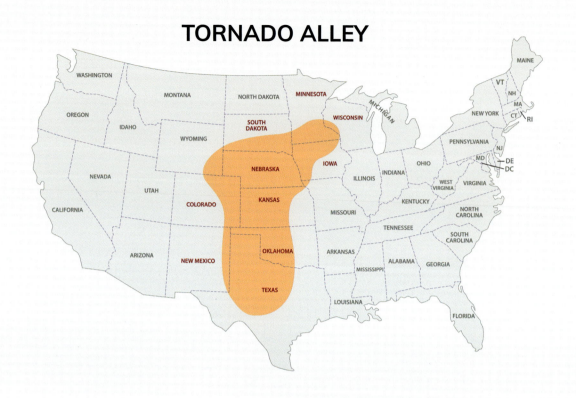

Most of the tornadoes in the United States happen in the Great Plains area. It has been nicknamed "Tornado Alley." Warm air travels north from the Gulf of Mexico. Cool, dry air travels south from Canada. They meet in Tornado Alley. It's the perfect mix of air to create tornadoes.

Tornadoes can happen at any time of year. They're more likely to occur during the warm spring and summer seasons.

An uncommon winter tornado in Illinois

TORNADO AFTERMATH

Tornadoes are dangerous. They can destroy neighborhoods. They can hurt or kill people. And they can strike with little warning.

Damage happens in two ways. The wind itself can be harmful. It can knock down trees or homes. Flying debris also causes problems. Tornadoes can throw things like rocks and boards at high speeds.

Tornadoes cause millions of dollars in damage. And they can leave people homeless. One of the worst tornadoes happened in Joplin, Missouri, in 2011. It caused nearly $2.8 billion in damage. It destroyed more than 7,000 buildings.

Trees and homes were flattened by the Joplin tornado.

Looking for personal items after the EF-5 tornado in Joplin, Missouri

In 2019, 1,517 tornadoes hit the United States. They caused 42 deaths. The next year was more deadly. There were only 1,075 tornadoes. But they killed about 76 people.

Tornado winds destroyed a neighborhood in Ohio in 2019.

Thousands of people in Bangladesh lost their homes due to the 1989 tornado.

The deadliest tornado in history took place in Bangladesh. In April 1989, a tornado touched down in two cities. It killed about 1,300 people. Another 12,000 people were hurt.

STAYING SAFE

Tornadoes can be hard to **predict**. Only about 20 percent of supercell storms form tornadoes. Scientists try to keep people safe. They study the weather. They send out warnings. Warnings tell people about storms.

A supercell storm

A siren that warns people about bad weather

A tornado watch means a tornado is possible in the area. A tornado warning means a tornado is in the area.

Tornadoes can be deadly. There are things you can do to stay safe. Know what to do ahead of time. Get a weather radio. It can keep you informed.

During a tornado, stay inside. Go to a basement. Or go to an **interior** room. Cover your head. Protect yourself from debris.

Students during a tornado drill at school

If you are in a car, stay put. Don't try to outrun a tornado. Keep your head down and covered. The storm will pass soon.

GLOSSARY

column (KAH-luhm)—something with a shape similar to a tall tube

debris (duh-BREE)—the scattered pieces of something that has been broken or destroyed

disaster (dih-ZASS-tuhr)—an event that causes much damage or suffering

Enhanced Fujita Scale (en-HANST foo-GEE-tuh SKALE)—a scale from one to five that uses tornado damage to find out how strong a tornado was

funnel (FUN-uhl)—a tube that narrows to a small opening at the bottom

interior (in-TEER-ee-uhr)—the inner part of something, such as a building

predict (prih-DIKT)—to say what you think will happen in the future

supercell (SOO-pur-sel)—an unusually large storm cell that contains strong upward movements of air

vortex (VOHR-tex)—air moving in a circular motion

waterspout (WAH-tur-spowt)—a tornado that forms or moves over water

READ MORE

Gibbons, Gail. *Tornadoes!* New York: Holiday House, 2019.

Rathburn, Betsy. *Tornadoes.* Minneapolis: Bellwether Media, Inc., 2020.

Shores, Lori. *How to Build a Tornado in a Bottle: A 4D Book.* North Mankato, MN: Capstone, 2018.

INTERNET SITES

Kiddle: "Tornado Facts for Kids"
kids.kiddle.co/Tornado

National Geographic Kids: "Tornado"
kids.nationalgeographic.com/science/article/tornado

Weather Wiz Kids: "Tornadoes"
weatherwizkids.com/?page_id=60

INDEX

Bangladesh, 25
categories, 14–15
color, 9
damage, 14, 20–25
duration, 10
Enhanced Fujita Scale, 14–15, 23
formation, 7
funnels, 4, 7, 13
Joplin tornado, 22–23
multiple vortex tornadoes, 13
names for tornadoes, 6
safety, 26–29

seasons, 19
sizes, 8
speed, 10, 14–15
supercells, 6, 26
temperatures, 7, 18
thunderstorms, 6
Tornado Alley, 18
tornado warnings, 26–27
tornado watches, 27
United States, 16, 24
water, 7, 9, 12
waterspouts, 12
wind, 7, 9, 14–15, 21

ABOUT THE AUTHOR

Jaclyn Jaycox is a children's book author and editor. When she's not writing, she loves reading and spending time with her family. She lives in southern Minnesota with her husband, two kids, and a spunky goldendoodle.